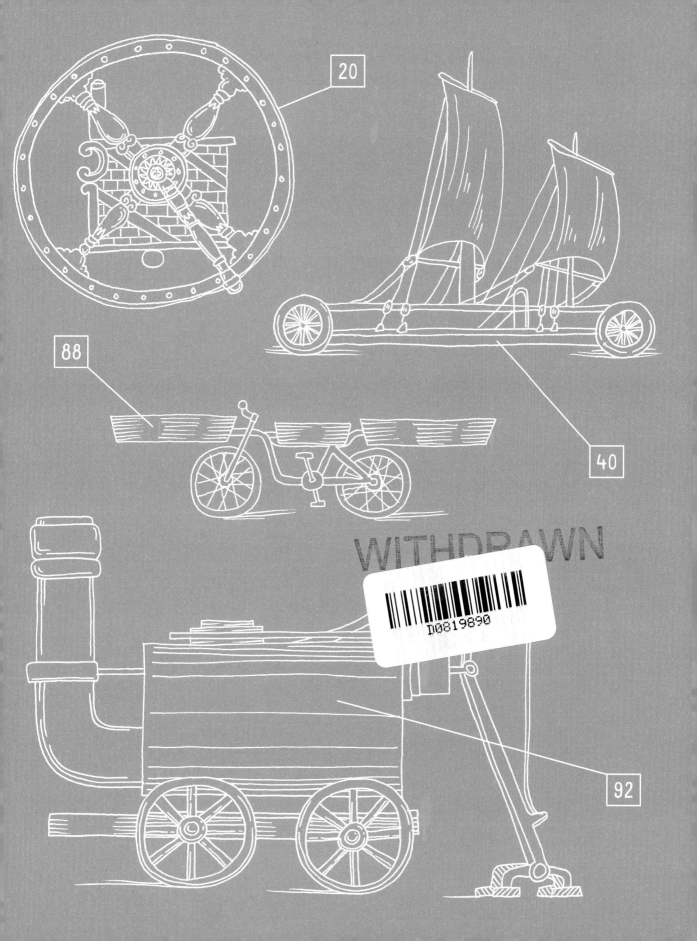

20

88

40

WITHDRAWN

D0819890

92

For Martka —MM

IMPOSSIBLE INVENTIONS

IDEAS THAT
SHOULDN'T WORK

Małgorzata Mycielska
Aleksandra and Daniel Mizieliński

Translated by Agnes Monod-Gayraud

GECKO PRESS

Why Do We Invent?

It begins with a dream or a need. A brilliant idea pops into the mind of a would-be inventor, or a person wants something that doesn't yet exist, and they work hard to bring it into being. We invent things to solve problems that are troubling us or to simplify our daily lives.

There's no rule about who can or can't be an inventor. It takes imagination, commitment and courage to push the limits of possibility. You never know when an idea will grow into something amazing and incredibly useful.

Perhaps you have an idea for an invention. People may make fun of it, but it takes a lot to come up with an original idea, even if it doesn't work out right away. It's always worth trying new ways of doing

things. If you don't try, you'll never know what fantastic things might have been! Even the greatest inventors in the world had a few hiccups along the way. Take Leonardo da Vinci, who lived 500 years ago. He came up with many contraptions that were extraordinary for the time, including a car, a helicopter, a hang-glider, a parachute, a submarine, an elevator, a telescope, a robotic knight—even a pair of shoes for walking on water!

Only a few of his inventions were built in his lifetime. Most couldn't be made because people didn't yet have access to the right materials. Da Vinci's ideas were often far ahead of their time—people didn't realize how handy a submarine, truck or helicopter could be.

flying machine

parachute

wind-up cart

tank

Leonardo da Vinci

In those days, he was probably considered a madman. Today, no one doubts his genius, or how much we owe him. What if he'd given up before he got started?

This book is full of daredevil inventors. Some of their inventions will amaze you, others will seem downright silly. At the heart of each one there are three things:

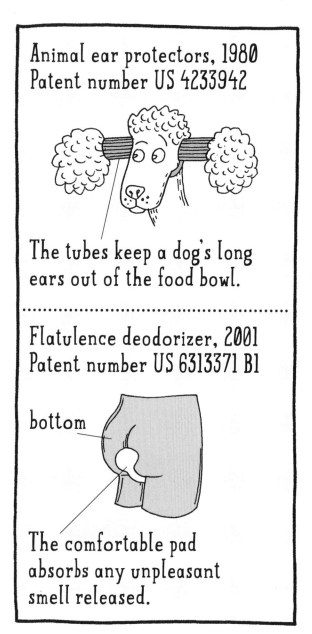

Animal ear protectors, 1980
Patent number US 4233942

The tubes keep a dog's long ears out of the food bowl.

Flatulence deodorizer, 2001
Patent number US 6313371 B1

bottom

The comfortable pad absorbs any unpleasant smell released.

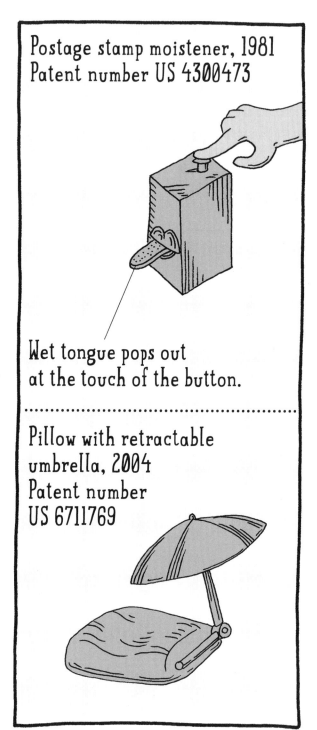

Postage stamp moistener, 1981
Patent number US 4300473

Wet tongue pops out at the touch of the button.

Pillow with retractable umbrella, 2004
Patent number US 6711769

creativity, passion and dedication. Imagine how boring the world would be without inventors! And how we'd miss their handy devices that we use every day.

In the 19th century, technological development was gaining speed, with more new machines created during this period than the previous centuries. Leading the way were engineers (from the Latin *in-geniosus*, meaning "gifted with genius," "clever," "ingenious"). As specialists across a range of fields, engineers came up with the most important inventions of the age. Around the same time, patent offices were established so inventors could patent their discoveries. An invention doesn't have to be remarkable to receive a patent—it can be anything from a child's toy to a rocket ship. It does have to be original, functional and able to be made. If the experts in the patent office decide an invention meets those requirements,

they will issue a patent. This gives the inventor exclusive rights to the idea for a certain period (usually around twenty years). It means he or she can produce and share the invention with others— or make money by selling it. When the patent expires, anyone can use the idea, and it's time for the inventor to come up with another one. And that's progress!

Automatic Temple Doors 1ST CENTURY CE

To open the doors, the priest must light a fire on the altar.

Rotating rods below the floor are attached to the temple doors.

rotating rods

A weight keeps the doors shut when the bucket is empty.

empty bucket

cistern full of water

Today, we're not surprised to see doors sliding open as we approach stores, office buildings, museums and airports. It doesn't occur to us to think this supernatural. The science of the light sensor has been part of our everyday lives for over half a century.

Yet two thousand years ago, people would have found an automatic door amazing and even terrifying. The design for the first self-opening door was devised and recorded by Heron of Alexandria, a Greek mathematician, physicist, inventor and engineer. He kept the details of his automatic temple doors secret, so the best explanation people could come up with at the time was that an invisible god was at work.

1. The fire on the altar heats the air in the cistern below.

4. As the rods turn, they open the doors to the temple.

2. The warm air expands and pushes the water out of the cistern and into the bucket.

3. The bucket, now full of water, puts tension on the rope, making the rods turn.

When the fire goes out, the temperature in the cistern drops and the water flows back into it. Once the bucket is empty, the weight on the other end of the rope turns the rods back again, and the doors close.

Passenger Dragon

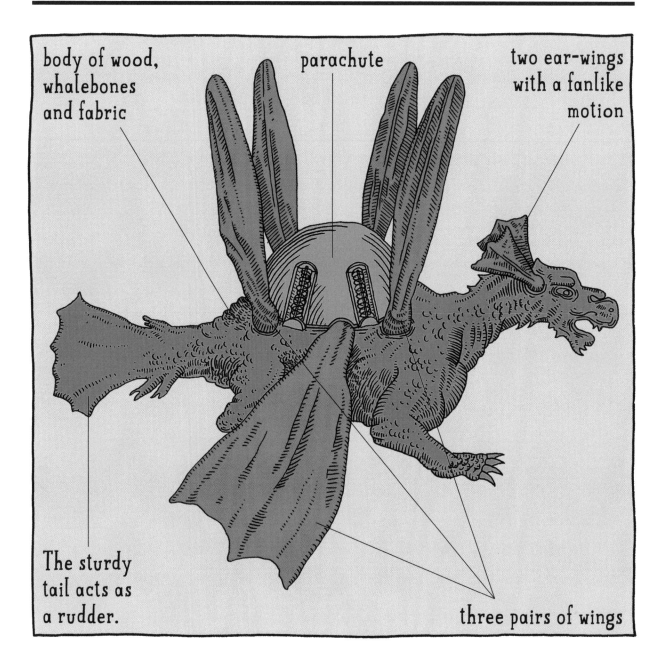

body of wood, whalebones and fabric

parachute

two ear-wings with a fanlike motion

The sturdy tail acts as a rudder.

three pairs of wings

One frosty February morning a long, long time ago in the city of Warsaw, a dragon flew over the Royal Castle. It sounds like a fairy tale, but it's true. Yet the dragon wasn't quite what you'd expect—it was made entirely from metal and wood. The mechanical dragon was the brainchild of Tito Livio Burattini, an Italian architect and inventor living in Poland in the 17th century. His first model, which was only about the length of a bicycle, was a prototype for the bigger and more complex fly-ing machine he planned to build next. Burattini arranged to test-fly the dragon before Poland's King Vladislav IV Vasa and his court.

The parachute uses springs to open and shut.

Two pilots wind up the mechanism that sets the wings in motion.

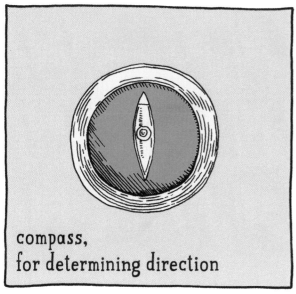

compass,
for determining direction

Burattini hoped to impress the king and receive a generous royal grant to finance his next high-flying project.

With only a cat on board, and powered by a makeshift engine of wheels, levers and springs, the dragon's first flight was a reasonable success. Not so the second. Something went awry and the dragon plunged to the ground. Undaunted, the inventor went on improving his project. But Burattini never managed to build the ultimate version of his mechanical drag-on. No matter how he tweaked the design, it was too heavy to get off the ground.

Bubble Messenger

The sender attaches wires to individual letters.

The letter with fewer bubbles arrives before the letter with more bubbles.

This machine might have looked like a sorcerer's apparatus. Someone expecting a message would peer into the bubbling cistern and write down the symbols that appeared within it. But this method of sending messages with bubbles wasn't for the wizard's lair—it was everyday practice at the local post office at the start of the 19th century.

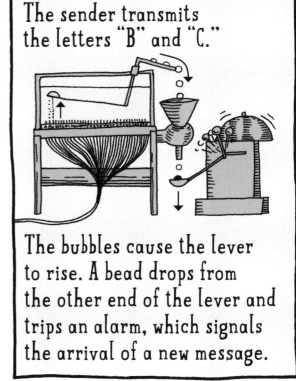

The sender transmits the letters "B" and "C."

The bubbles cause the lever to rise. A bead drops from the other end of the lever and trips an alarm, which signals the arrival of a new message.

The bubble messenger was invented over 200 years ago by Samuel Thomas von Sömmerring, a German physicist and doctor.

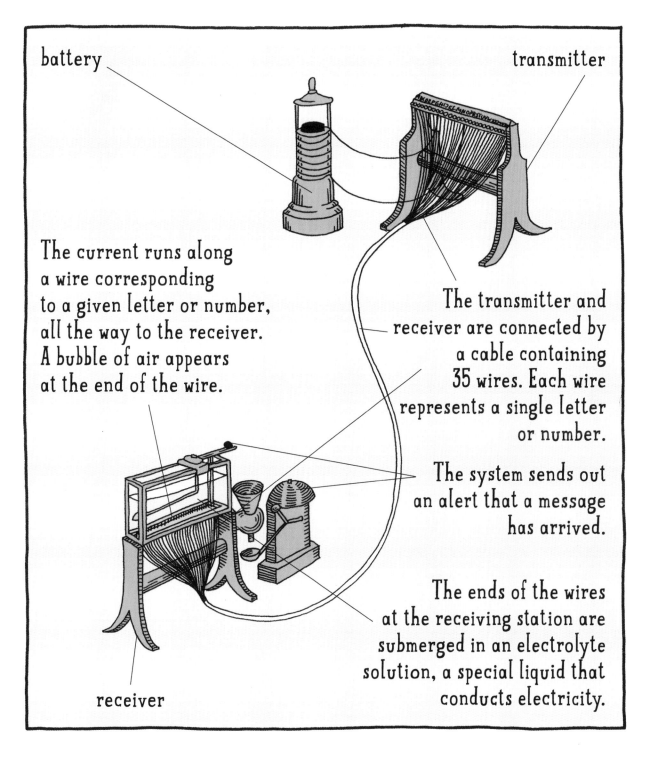

battery

transmitter

The current runs along a wire corresponding to a given letter or number, all the way to the receiver. A bubble of air appears at the end of the wire.

The transmitter and receiver are connected by a cable containing 35 wires. Each wire represents a single letter or number.

The system sends out an alert that a message has arrived.

The ends of the wires at the receiving station are submerged in an electrolyte solution, a special liquid that conducts electricity.

receiver

He came up with one of the first and certainly one of the strangest means of long-distance communication: the electrochemical telegraph.

Sömmering's telegraph wasn't popular. Firstly, it didn't work if the sender and receiver were too far apart. Secondly, it took far too long to decipher messages.

19

Wheel Carriage

What do you get if you combine a Ferris wheel with a giant hamster wheel? The chosen vehicle of the Holy Roman Emperor Maximilian I!

His invention consisted of a rolling wheel powered by human muscle. It was an ambitious concept, and not very practical. That's probably why it was never built.

Maximilian I dreamed up huge parades of bizarre vehicles. Alas, he couldn't afford to bring them about, so to cheer himself up he commissioned Albrecht Dürer to draw his wildest ideas.

More than 500 years ago, he ruled over half of Europe, so he was on the move. Perhaps bored with horse-drawn carriages, he thought up a novel way to get around.

It existed only in the emperor's imagination—until he shared his idea with one of the most brilliant artists of the day, Albrecht Dürer, who made detailed

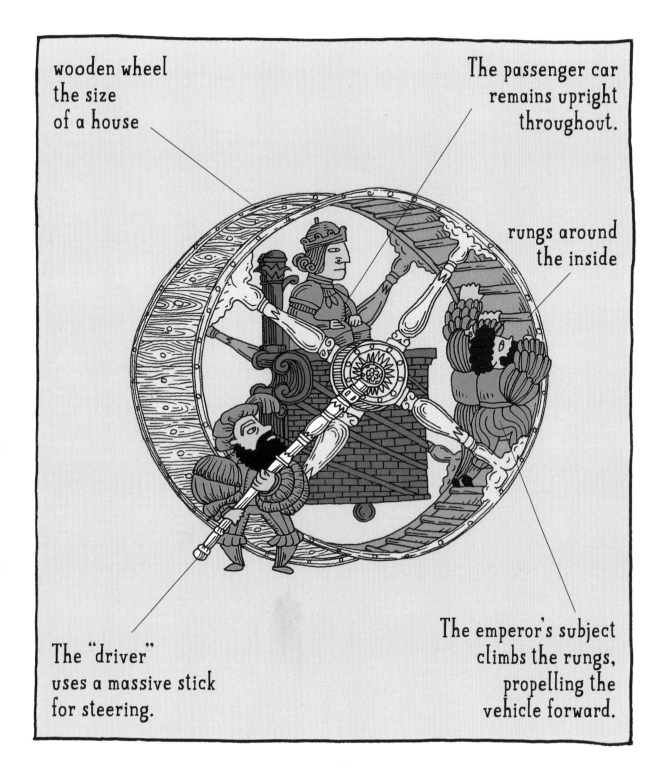

wooden wheel
the size
of a house

The passenger car
remains upright
throughout.

rungs around
the inside

The "driver"
uses a massive stick
for steering.

The emperor's subject
climbs the rungs,
propelling the
vehicle forward.

sketches of the fanciful vehicle. Imagine cruising along today's highways in one of these wheel carriages—one person scrabbling up the sides to make it go faster while the passengers lounge comfortably in the chair. One thing's for sure—a ride like that could never get boring!

23

Robotic Chess Master

When IBM's Deep Blue machine defeated world champion Garry Kasparov in a chess game in 1997, it was a leap forward for computing.

It was built by Hungarian philosopher and engineer Wolfgang von Kempelen, who presented his contraption at the court of Empress Maria Theresa of Austria.

A voice box allows the Turk to declare "Check!"

box supposed to house the machinery, but serves no real purpose

lever that doesn't actually wind anything

small, numbered dial, for communicating with the chess player inside

But Deep Blue wasn't the first machine to have beaten a man at the game. Its predecessor in the 18th century was known as the "Mechanical Turk" or the "Turk".

He was hailed as the greatest inventor in the empire. People believed that the Turk was an automaton or "thinking machine."

Kempelen embarked on a tour of Europe with his invention, challenging the best chess players across the continent to beat the Turk.

It was a fascinating contraption, and Kempelen and his associates managed to keep its secret for over 60 years, as they toured Europe and the Americas.

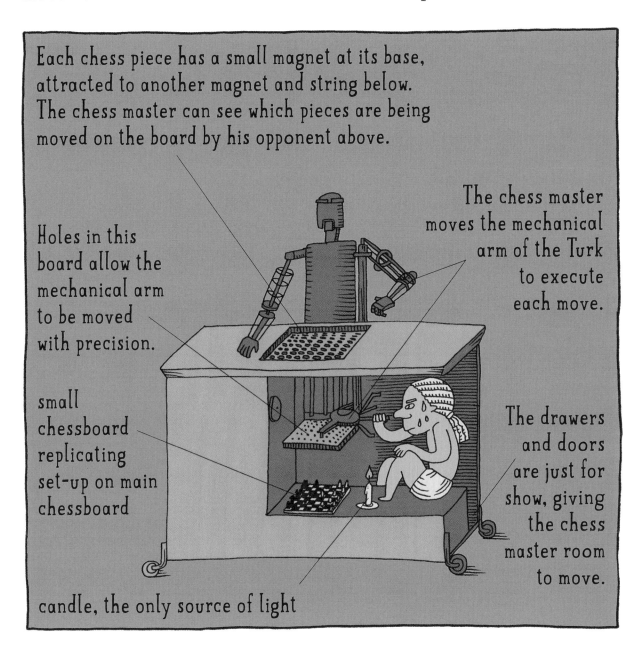

Each chess piece has a small magnet at its base, attracted to another magnet and string below. The chess master can see which pieces are being moved on the board by his opponent above.

The chess master moves the mechanical arm of the Turk to execute each move.

Holes in this board allow the mechanical arm to be moved with precision.

small chessboard replicating set-up on main chessboard

The drawers and doors are just for show, giving the chess master room to move.

candle, the only source of light

Even Napoleon Bonaparte tried his luck —to no avail. The machine was almost impossible to beat, losing only six of its 300-odd matches.

In 1834 a French newspaper disclosed that a human chess master was hidden inside the machine, controlling its movements and outplaying its opponents.

Bird Ship

Just over three centuries ago, King John V of Portugal received a letter containing the description and sketches for an airship called the Passarola (meaning "bird" in Portuguese). Bartolemeu de Gusmão, a scholar from Brazil, asked for funding from the king, and the 18th-century equivalent of a patent on his invention. He also demanded absolute secrecy.

balloon made of paper

A flame heats the air inside the balloon.

Before Gusmão began building his airship, he held a presentation especially for the king. Reports from that day suggest that the Passarola was meant to function like a hot air balloon.

The king agreed at once to the inventor's requests. Although the original document still exists, many details of the invention remain a mystery. Perhaps because Gusmão was afraid his idea would be stolen, he omitted details in his description, and added a few useless ones to confuse a would-be spy.

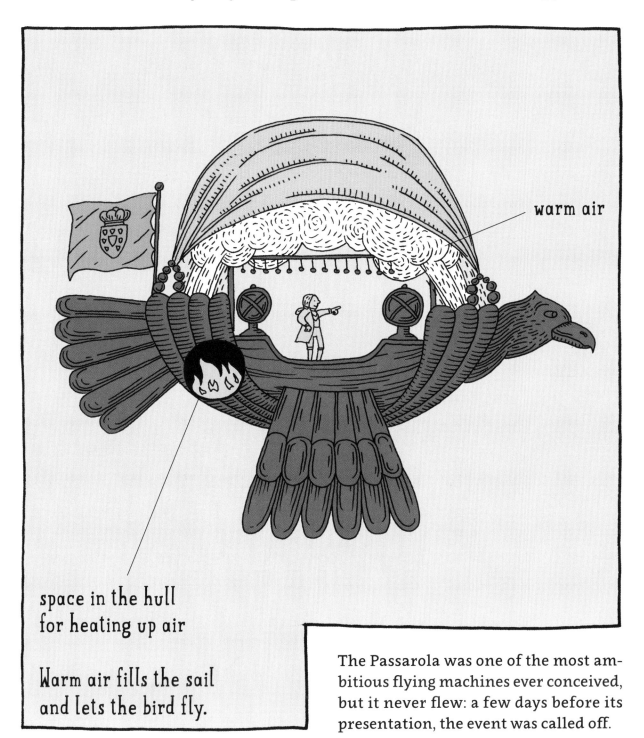

warm air

space in the hull
for heating up air

Warm air fills the sail
and lets the bird fly.

The Passarola was one of the most ambitious flying machines ever conceived, but it never flew: a few days before its presentation, the event was called off.

Personal Cloud Maker

A device that produces bad weather—why would anyone invent such a thing? Well, clouds could be one tool in the battle against global warming. As the ozone layer thins because of greenhouse gas emissions, clouds provide a way to protect Earth from the sun's damaging ultraviolet rays. They're like a parasol for the planet.

Some scientists are exploring a technique called "cloud brightening," which changes the make-up of clouds to make them more reflective and so bounce more of the sun's radiation back into space.

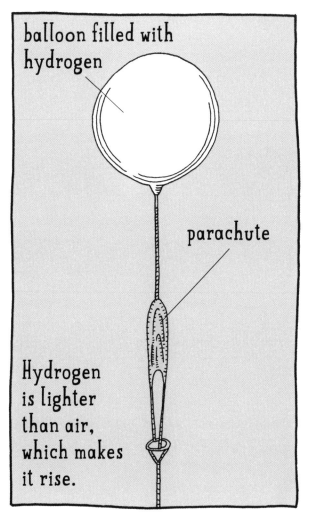

balloon filled with hydrogen

parachute

Hydrogen is lighter than air, which makes it rise.

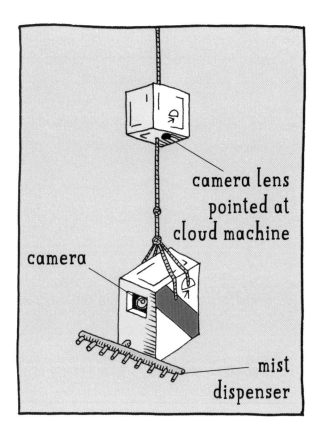

camera lens pointed at cloud machine

camera

mist dispenser

Based on these principles, the New York artist Karolina Sobecka invented her very own cloud machine. Using her device, anyone can whip up their own bit of cloud. However, the inventor has some tweaking yet to do on her design in order to produce a decent variety and range of cloud cover.

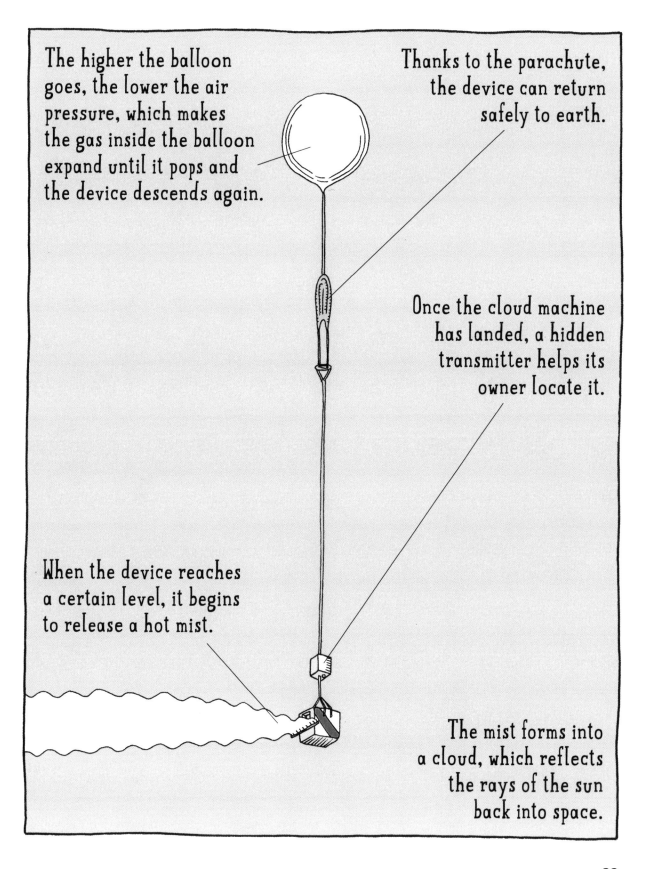

The higher the balloon goes, the lower the air pressure, which makes the gas inside the balloon expand until it pops and the device descends again.

Thanks to the parachute, the device can return safely to earth.

Once the cloud machine has landed, a hidden transmitter helps its owner locate it.

When the device reaches a certain level, it begins to release a hot mist.

The mist forms into a cloud, which reflects the rays of the sun back into space.

33

Water Clock

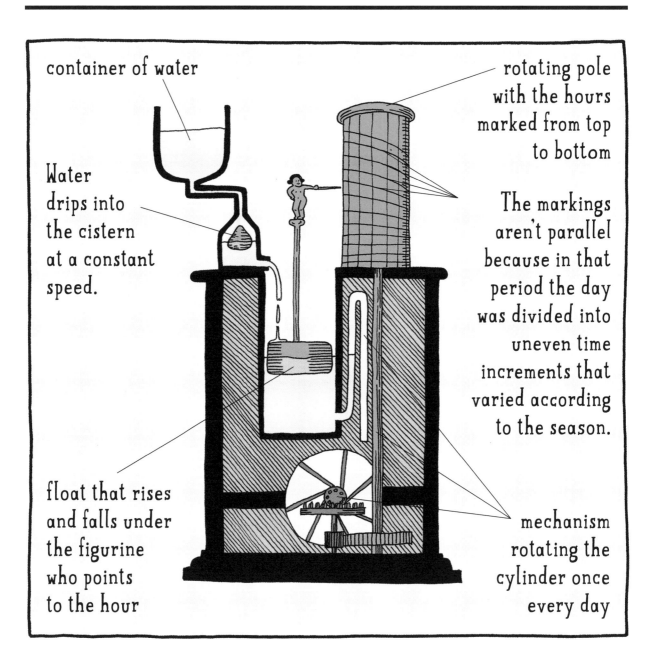

container of water

rotating pole with the hours marked from top to bottom

Water drips into the cistern at a constant speed.

The markings aren't parallel because in that period the day was divided into uneven time increments that varied according to the season.

float that rises and falls under the figurine who points to the hour

mechanism rotating the cylinder once every day

There's a saying that time flows like a river. And, as it turns out, the earliest clocks used the flow of water to measure time: water dripping from one pot into another, for example. Unfortunately, they weren't very precise because their inventors couldn't ensure a steady flow of water through the device. That is, until two thousand years ago, when the Greek inventor Ctesibius improved the accuracy of the water clock with his version of the clepsydra or "water thief."

This was a complicated but very precise clock. Later, his invention was further enhanced with "special effects" such as mechanisms that made a figurine

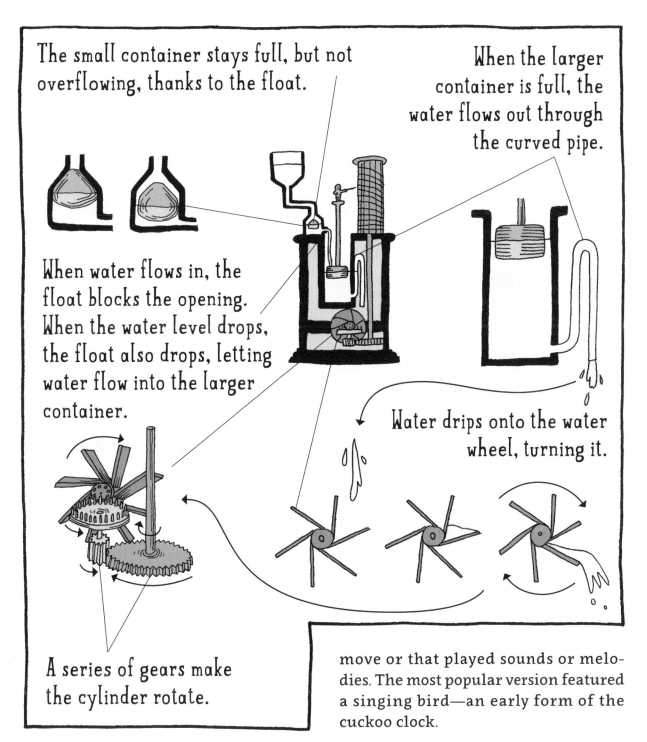

The small container stays full, but not overflowing, thanks to the float.

When the larger container is full, the water flows out through the curved pipe.

When water flows in, the float blocks the opening. When the water level drops, the float also drops, letting water flow into the larger container.

Water drips onto the water wheel, turning it.

A series of gears make the cylinder rotate.

move or that played sounds or melodies. The most popular version featured a singing bird—an early form of the cuckoo clock.

39

Land Yacht

The world's first land yacht was invented over 400 years ago by the Flemish engineer and mathematician Simon Stevin, for Prince Maurice of Orange.

A combination of sailboat and carriage, it was the first wind-powered land vehicle. It could travel at a dizzying speed for that time—almost three times that of a horse-drawn coach.

Stevin's first trial was held on a beach in Holland. It failed when a strong gust toppled the vehicle. The inventor increased the ballast to provide more stability. This adjustment made the land yacht fully functional.

Soon a regular connection was set up between two seaside towns. Each one-way trip took about two hours.

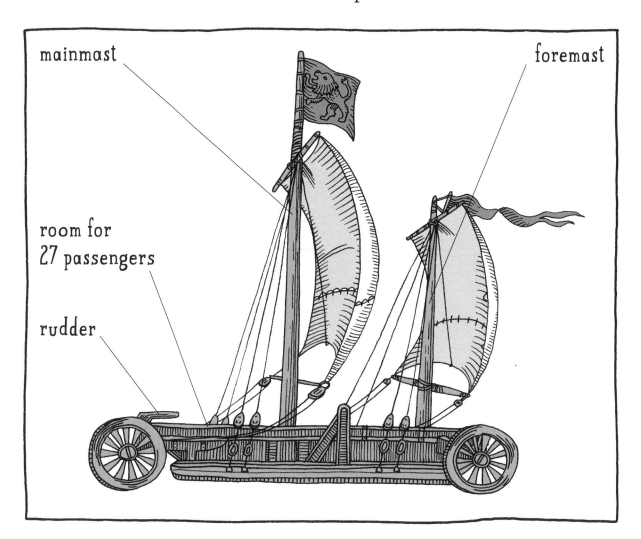

mainmast

foremast

room for
27 passengers

rudder

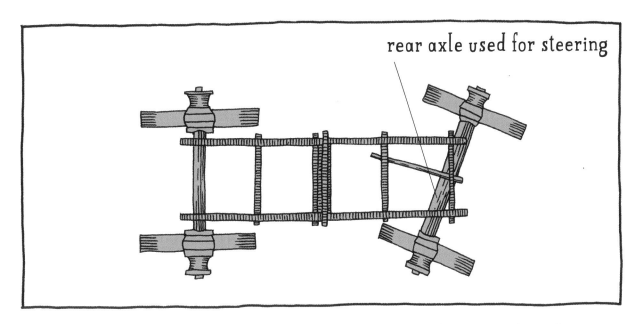

rear axle used for steering

Land yachts are still around today. They are reminiscent of Stevin's model, but smaller, for a single person.
Land sailing (or sand yachting) has been an official racing sport since the 1950s. Thanks to technological improvements, today's land yachts can reach up to 200 km per hour (124 mph).

More recently, scientists have proposed using the same idea to power discovery vehicles on other planets, including a wind-powered rover.

42

Wireless Power Generator

Was he crazy or a genius? It's still unclear which best describes Serbian–American inventor Nikola Tesla. After immigrating to the United States in 1884, he set up several laboratories to develop and test his ideas, ultimately patenting around 125 inventions. His many ideas included wireless communication, x-ray, a radio-controlled torpedo for the navy, and a way of electrifying school-children to make them smarter. He also claimed to have contacted extra-terrestrials. Most fascinating was his vision for free energy. Tesla was convinced that electricity could be conducted wirelessly all over the world—at no cost. It would travel without electrical outlets or cables directly via Earth's surface.

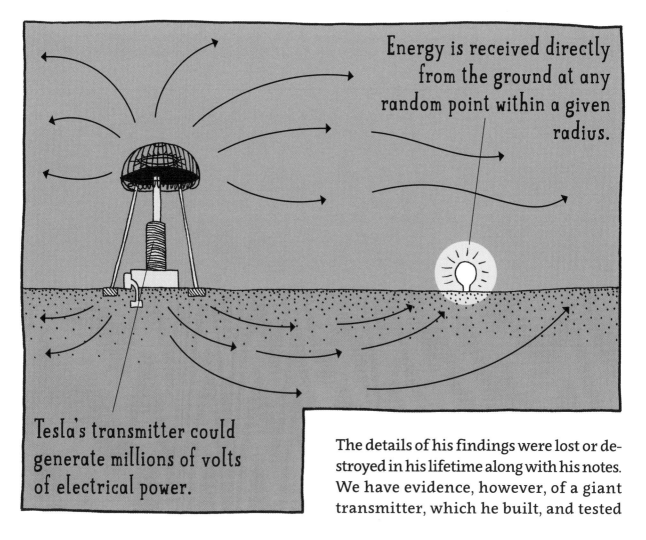

Energy is received directly from the ground at any random point within a given radius.

Tesla's transmitter could generate millions of volts of electrical power.

The details of his findings were lost or destroyed in his lifetime along with his notes. We have evidence, however, of a giant transmitter, which he built, and tested

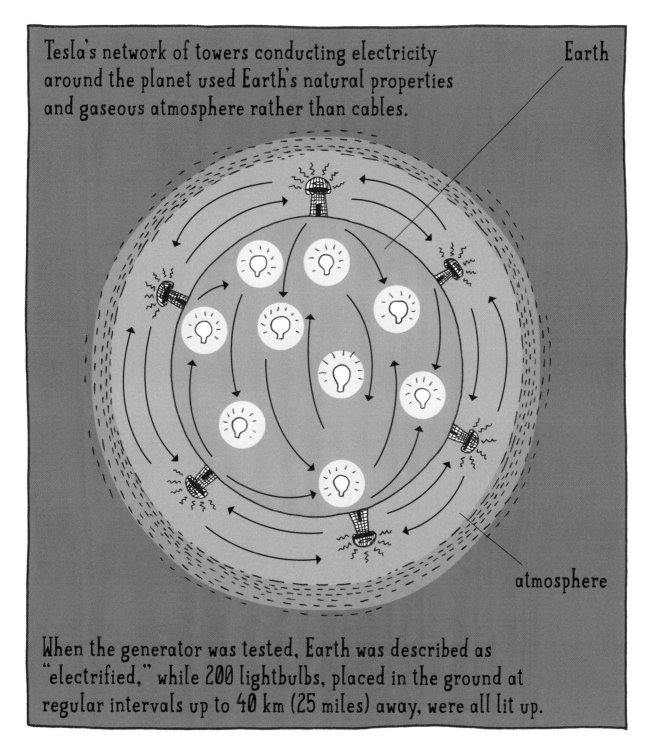

Tesla's network of towers conducting electricity around the planet used Earth's natural properties and gaseous atmosphere rather than cables.

Earth

atmosphere

When the generator was tested, Earth was described as "electrified," while 200 lightbulbs, placed in the ground at regular intervals up to 40 km (25 miles) away, were all lit up.

in front of an audience—twice. Towards the end of his life, Tesla's erratic conduct led people to call him a madman. They didn't allow him to conduct any more experiments. The famous inventor died penniless. Or, perhaps, as some have suggested, he took a trip in his very last invention: a time machine.

Steam Horse

The cab design allows the operator to drive the vehicle while carrying out duties such as collecting fares.

A light at the front means the vehicle can be seen at night.

connection for the passenger wagon

In the late 19th century, a bus (or omnibus, as it was called) was commonly pulled by horses. But steam-powered vehicles were beginning to appear as well. (By then, steam engines were widely used in boats and rail locomotives.) Although steam technology made travel faster and cheaper, it took a long time for people to warm up to the idea. The billowing steam was said to frighten horses and aggravate dogs, to make ladies faint and small children fall ill.

were undeterred. American inventor S. R. Mathewson came up with an elegant solution: his steam locomotive was designed to look like a horse-drawn carriage.

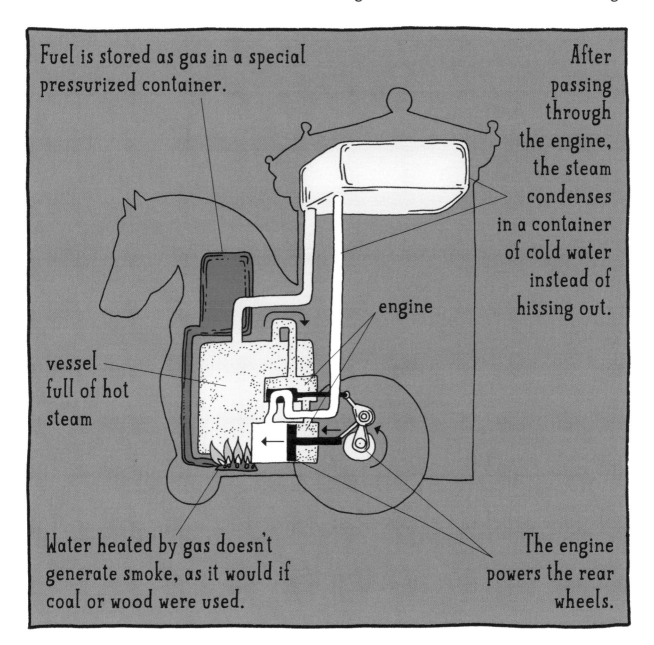

Fuel is stored as gas in a special pressurized container.

After passing through the engine, the steam condenses in a container of cold water instead of hissing out.

engine

vessel full of hot steam

Water heated by gas doesn't generate smoke, as it would if coal or wood were used.

The engine powers the rear wheels.

Some even believed that the diabolical machines stopped cows and hens from producing milk and laying eggs. But those willing to go with the spirit of the times

The steam horse blended perfectly into the 19th-century cityscape. Today, too, it would fit in just fine...at a carnival, at least!

50

51

Running Bike

The cyclist is harnessed to the frame with a sturdy strap.

handle bars

brake

A triangular notch in the frame serves as a footrest.

strong, lightweight frame

A frame, two wheels and handlebars—that's all there is to the "Fliz." It's essentially a bike for running, since it has no pedals. Designed quite recently in Germany by Tom Hambrock and Juri Spetter, it was inspired by Karl Drais's invention of 200 years earlier. Drais's Laufmaschine (running machine), nicknamed the "dandy horse," had two wheels connected to a

DANDY HORSE 1817

The rotating fork for steering was a novelty for the period.

FLIZ 2012

frame, with handlebars and a seat. To get it going, cyclists had to push against the ground with their feet. The Fliz operates on the same principle, yet its design is thoroughly modern. The faster you run, the quicker it glides. When you really get going, you can lift your feet and feel you're almost flying!

Balloon Boat

Everything has its own weight, even air. An inflated balloon falls because of the weight of the rubber it's made of and the air inside it. For a balloon to float, it has to be filled with something lighter than ordinary air. For example, warm air, which has less density, and therefore less weight, than cool air. Or helium, a gas that's lighter than air.

The same applies to balloons for transport, which people started flying in the 18th century. They were propelled by hot air until helium was identified in the following century.

Francesco Lana de Terzi—an Italian priest, mathematician and physicist who lived over 300 years ago—had neither of these solutions at his disposal. He had to work out for himself how to realize his wild dream: to build a boat so light it could fly. His solution: vacuum balloons.

His invention was a great idea, but impossible to implement. The copper sheets he planned to use for the balloons were too heavy.

To this day, we haven't found the right material for such a balloon: sufficiently airtight to have all the air sucked out of it and maintain a vacuum, light enough to rise into the air, and rigid enough to retain its shape and withstand pressure from the air around it. Still, a copper balloon boat is a fantastic idea!

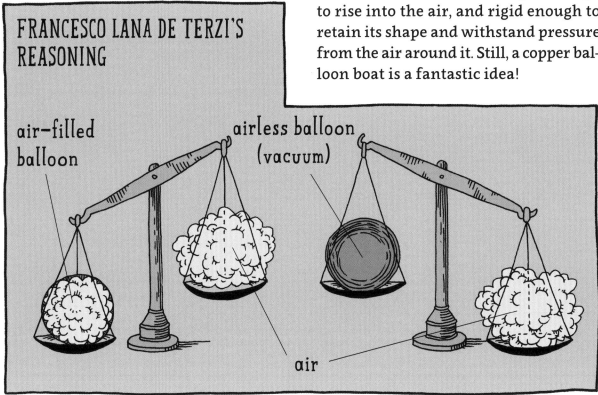

FRANCESCO LANA DE TERZI'S REASONING

air-filled balloon

airless balloon (vacuum)

air

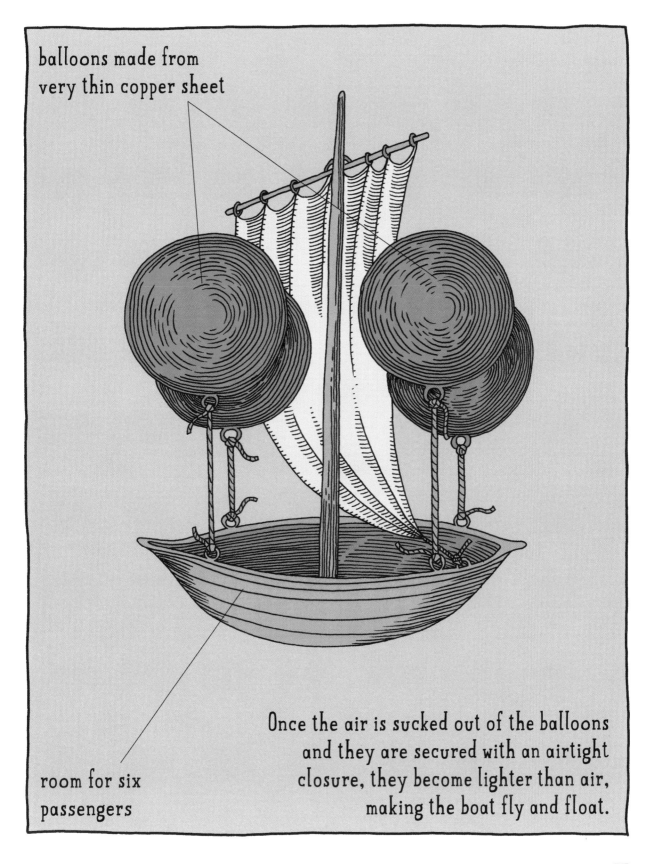

balloons made from
very thin copper sheet

room for six
passengers

Once the air is sucked out of the balloons
and they are secured with an airtight
closure, they become lighter than air,
making the boat fly and float.

58

Trust humans to make a boat sail into the sky.

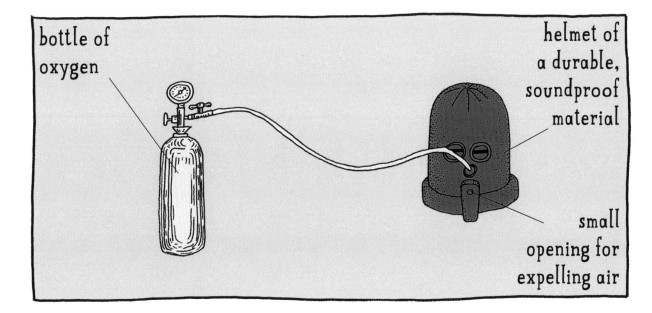

bottle of oxygen

helmet of a durable, soundproof material

small opening for expelling air

The American science-fiction writer and inventor Hugo Gernsback was known for some truly startling inventions. Among his eighty or so patents was a device for studying while asleep and another for contacting aliens.

Gernsback's ideas ranged from bizarre to brilliant: he invented a device for hear-

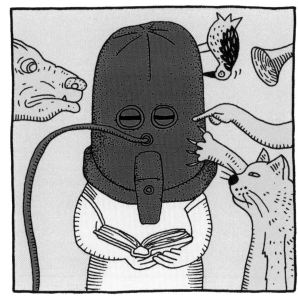

ing through the teeth; he also insisted that teleportation was inevitable and speculated that we would all one day wear "teleyeglasses."

The "Isolator" shut out life's distractions, allowing the wearer to focus on a single task. A noisy street, a dog barking, the smell of dinner wafting in from the

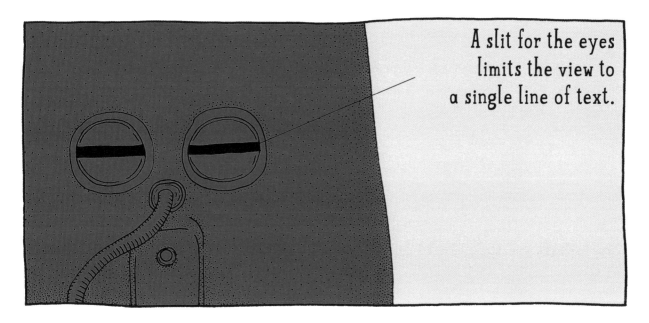

A slit for the eyes limits the view to a single line of text.

Gernsback had about a thousand ideas a minute, which he forgot unless he wrote them down. To overcome the problem, he invented a concentration helmet.

kitchen, light slanting through the window—all were held at bay when the helmet was on. Although it's unlikely that this wacky invention was ever produced.

62

All-terrain Travel Wheel

FIRST ATTEMPTS

The interior wheel remains stable thanks to three small rotating wheels.

At the end of the 19th century, most roads were unsealed dirt tracks, full of bumps and potholes, a serious obstacle to travel. Inventors around the world tried to come up with a vehicle that could cross any terrain. One common idea of the period was the monowheel. More than a dozen models were invented across Europe and the United States, the first built in 1869 by a French craftsman, Rousseau of Marseille. All had a common flaw, however: it was almost impossible to balance and steer a one-wheeled vehicle.

In 1883 the Polish engineer Stanisław Barycki added two more wheels to the monowheel design to make it sturdier. His model, named the "Swallow," was meant to tackle every obstacle with ease,

FAILED ATTEMPT AT WIND PROPULSION

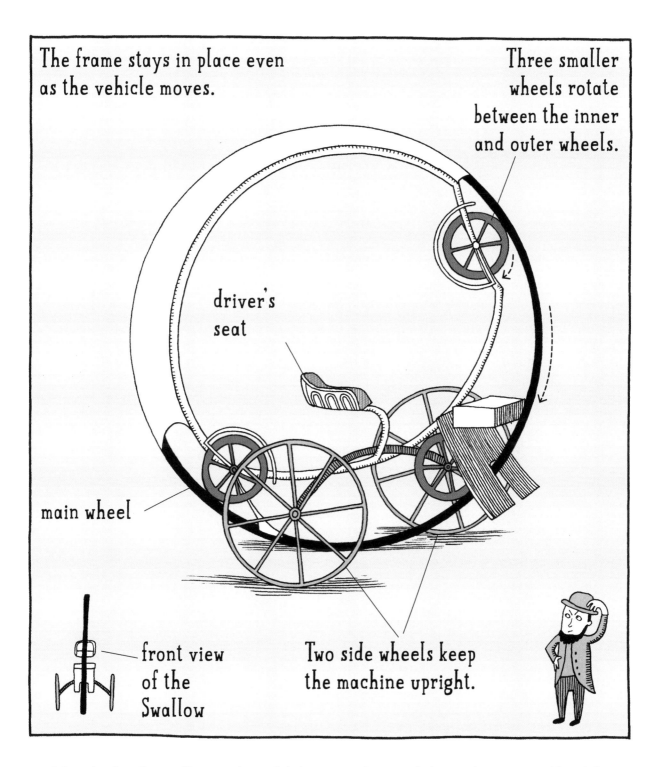

The frame stays in place even as the vehicle moves.

Three smaller wheels rotate between the inner and outer wheels.

driver's seat

main wheel

front view of the Swallow

Two side wheels keep the machine upright.

making it the first all-terrain vehicle. But although it rolled readily downhill, there was no way to propel the vehicle over flat or uneven ground. Barycki tried using pedals, and even a sail, without success. He spent his fortune testing his invention but couldn't come up with a final design that worked.

Eco Exerciser

Watching runners on the beach, Lebanese inventor Nadim Inaty thought about all the energy going to waste. He was inspired to design a power-generating treadmill called the "green wheel." A sort of human hamster wheel, it collects the kinetic energy produced when a person moves and converts it into electricity.

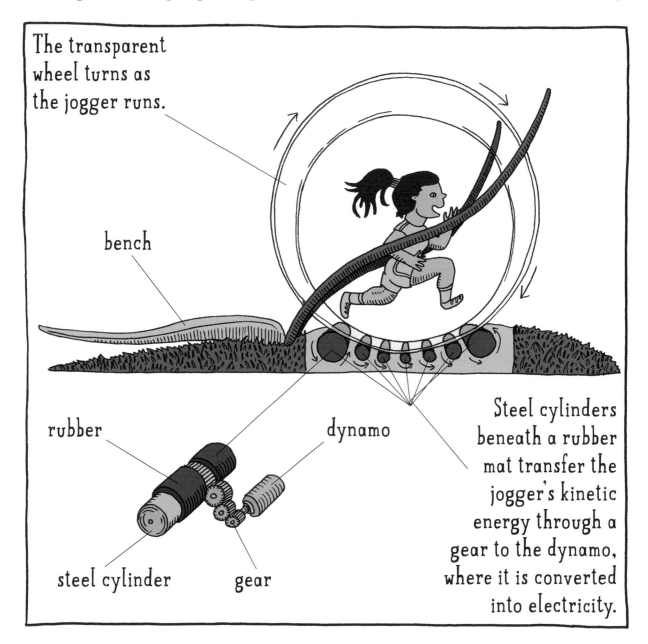

The transparent wheel turns as the jogger runs.

bench

rubber

dynamo

steel cylinder

gear

Steel cylinders beneath a rubber mat transfer the jogger's kinetic energy through a gear to the dynamo, where it is converted into electricity.

Inaty calculated that thirty minutes of exercise would generate enough energy to power a light bulb for five hours, or to charge a laptop or twelve mobile phones. The combined energy of a dozen or so wheels could keep street lamps and traffic lights running. Best of all, the process involves clean energy, meaning it creates no pollution, and it's free!

Inaty proposed setting up these "green-power wheels" in cities around the world to help supply their energy. It would be ideal in his home city of Beirut, where there are frequent power shortages. How would a few wheels go in your neighbourhood? Wouldn't it be great to get some exercise and power your community at the same time?

Safety bars lock the wheel until the runner is ready.

Lowered bars keep the runner from falling out.

Pressing the bars down stops the wheel.

Bird Suit

Ever since the story of Daedalus and Icarus, people have fantasized about taking to the sky with wings.

For thousands of years people have been trying to build wings that would allow us to fly like birds. Among the most dedicated in their attempts to fashion wings for humans was Reuben Jasper Spalding of the United States. His flying machine was essentially an upgrade of Leonardo da Vinci's ornithopter, sketched 400 years earlier.

Spalding patented his design towards the end of the 19th century, after submitting a

Leonardo da Vinci

The feathers can be made from various materials.

leather harness attached to the body

The spring action means the wearer only has to push the wings down and they lift back up on their own.

series of fascinating drawings and notes. On paper, the contraption looked convincing. But it would never get off the ground. The wings weighed at least as much as a person; simply putting them on was no mean feat. Still, the inventor was sure that one day his ornithopter would take humans up into the clouds.

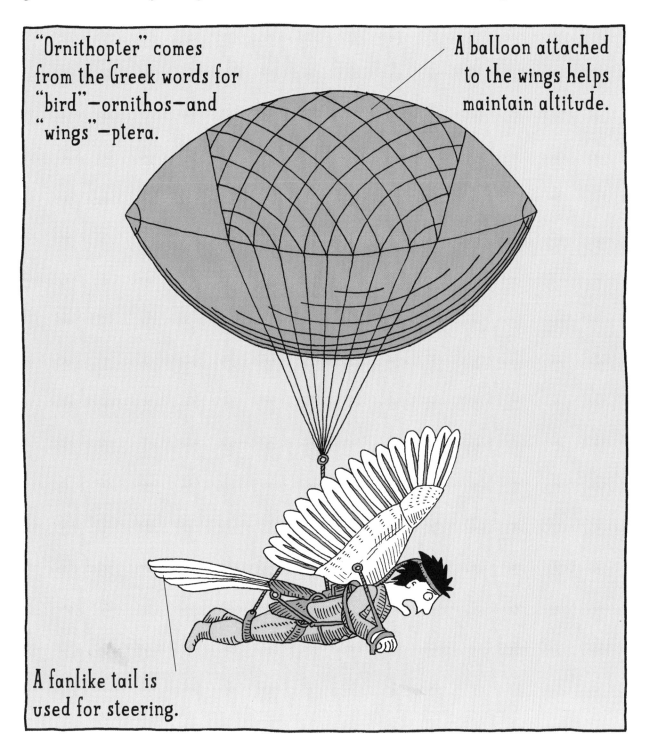

"Ornithopter" comes from the Greek words for "bird"—ornithos—and "wings"—ptera.

A balloon attached to the wings helps maintain altitude.

A fanlike tail is used for steering.

74

Candle Clocks

How did people measure time before mechanical clocks were invented? For over four thousand years, people used natural phenomena to help them determine the time of day, such as the shadow cast upon a sun dial (1), water dripping from one pot into another, or through a series of tubes and canisters (2), or grains of sand flowing through an hourglass (3).

About two thousand years ago candle clocks began to appear, although we can't say precisely when, nor who invented them.

1. SUN DIAL

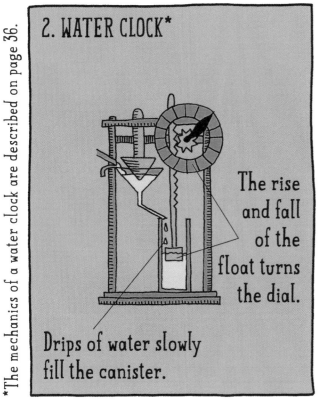

2. WATER CLOCK*

The rise and fall of the float turns the dial.

Drips of water slowly fill the canister.

*The mechanics of a water clock are described on page 36.

3. HOURGLASS

Sand moves steadily from the upper bulb to the lower.

GRADUATED CANDLE

The candle was divided into sections for the activities of the day. King Alfred the Great of England was known to use this "clock" in the 9th century.

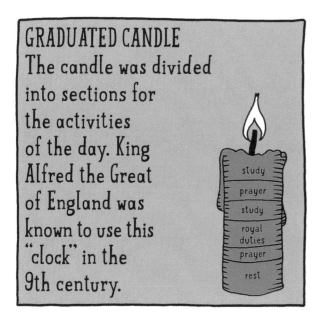

SCENTED CANDLE

Invented in ancient China, the candle was made with layers of incense. When the scent was released it was time for the next activity.

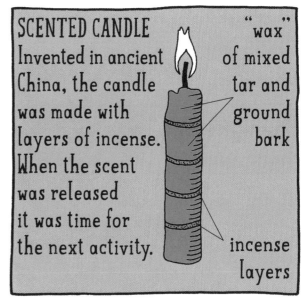

"wax" of mixed tar and ground bark

incense layers

ALARM CLOCK CANDLE

When enough wax drips away, each metal piece clatters onto the plate below. This is the origin of the phrase "to hear a pin drop."

MATCHSTICK CLOCK

flammable materials

metal beads

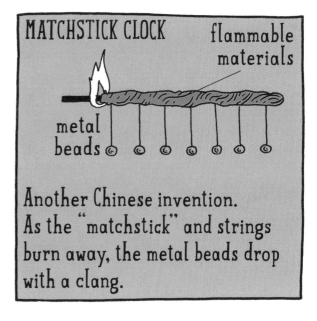

Another Chinese invention. As the "matchstick" and strings burn away, the metal beads drop with a clang.

OIL CLOCK

Used in the 15th century. As the oil burns, its level drops, with time indicated by the gauge on the container.

Candle clocks were simple to use, but there were drawbacks. They burned out quickly and had to be replaced often. So people continued to look for more sustainable ways to measure time.

Today, candles are cheap and plentiful, and candle clocks are quite easy to make. So next time you're bored on a rainy day, you might make your own.

79

Airborne Automobile

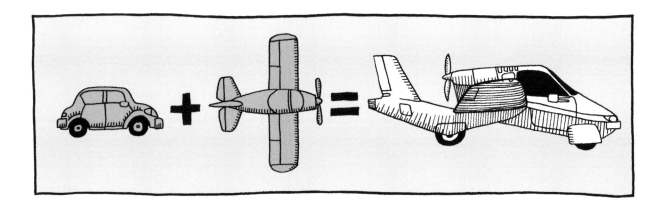

It's every inventor's dream to build a car that can also fly—and several have tried. One example is the ConvAirCar, built by Convair in 1947, based on a design by US engineer Ted Hall. It was a two-seat car attached beneath a removable plane (with wings, fuselage and engine). There were test flights, but Convair soon lost interest and dropped the idea.

Much more recently the idea has been brought back to life. And while it may look like an overblown toy or the work of a mad engineer, the world's first four-wheeled, twin-winged flying car is real. In other words, it's a dream come true! "Transition" was designed by a team of American scientists, pilots and engineers from a company called Terrafugia.

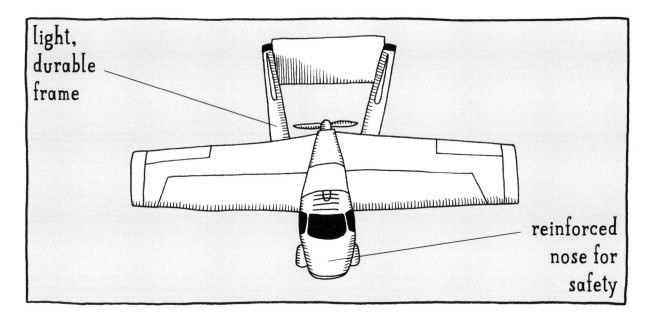

light, durable frame

reinforced nose for safety

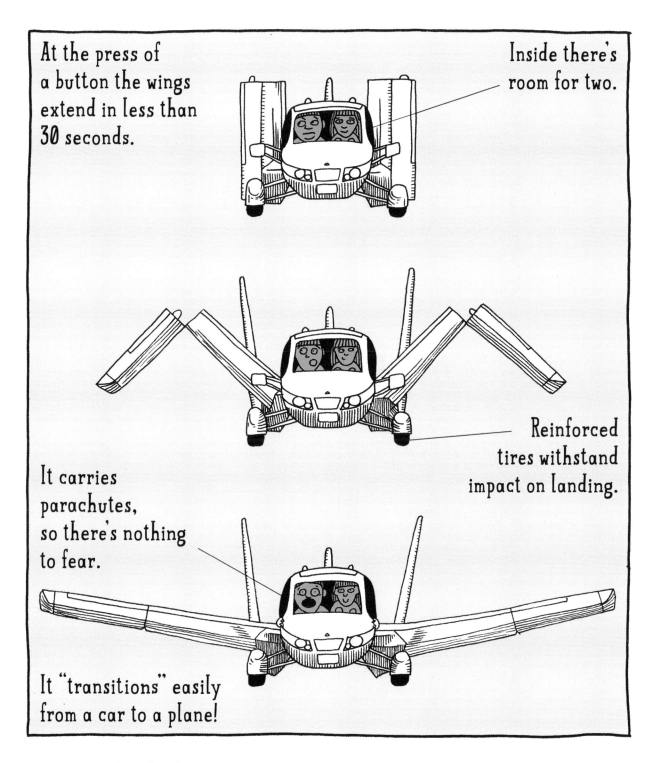

At the press of a button the wings extend in less than 30 seconds.

Inside there's room for two.

Reinforced tires withstand impact on landing.

It carries parachutes, so there's nothing to fear.

It "transitions" easily from a car to a plane!

It was certified for flight in 2009, and for the road in 2011. Flying at 185 km per hour (115 mph), it can zip from one major city to another in just a few hours. And it doesn't need stopovers—unless the pilots want to refuel at a local cafe. The best thing about Transition? You can park it in the street like an ordinary car.

82

Transport Cloud

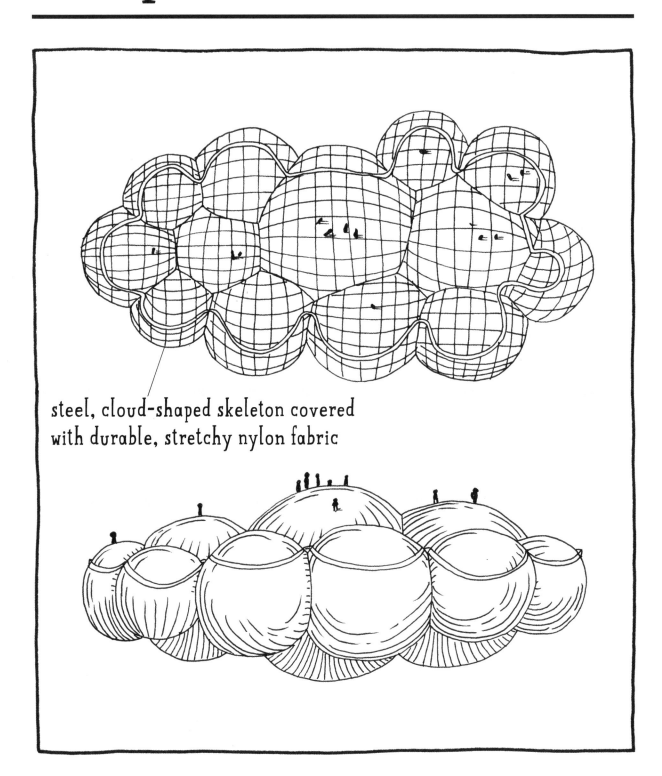

steel, cloud-shaped skeleton covered
with durable, stretchy nylon fabric

Have you ever thought how nice it would be to drift away on a cloud? No timetable, no ticket, no fixed destination. Leaving it all to the wind to determine where you'll go and how long it will take.

Tiago Barros, a Portuguese architect living in New York, dreamed of making this childhood dream a reality. He decided to invent a transport cloud.

So far, the concept he called "Passing Cloud" is a giant balloon filled with helium, a gas lighter than air. It's not for people in a hurry, as the direction, speed and destination of the cloud are all determined by the wind. But with no jet or petrol exhausts, it is pollution free. Passengers would have to wear special suits for warmth and carry oxygen tanks

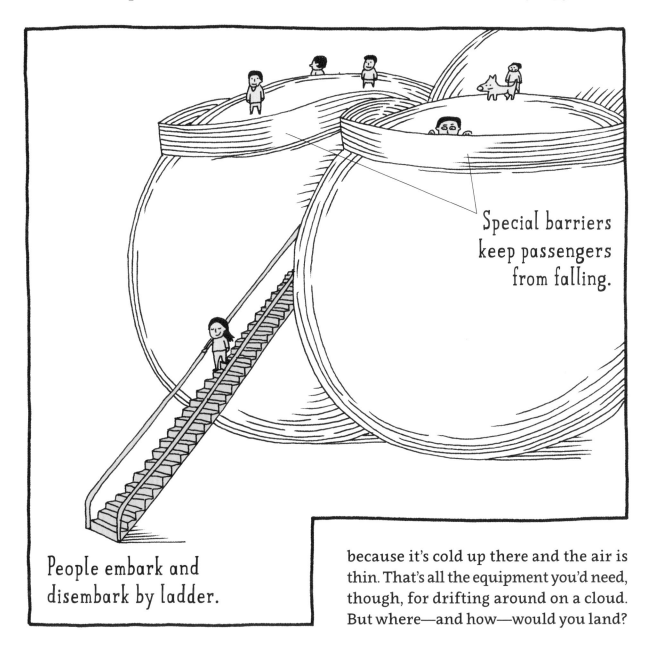

Special barriers keep passengers from falling.

People embark and disembark by ladder.

because it's cold up there and the air is thin. That's all the equipment you'd need, though, for drifting around on a cloud. But where—and how—would you land?

87

Aircycle

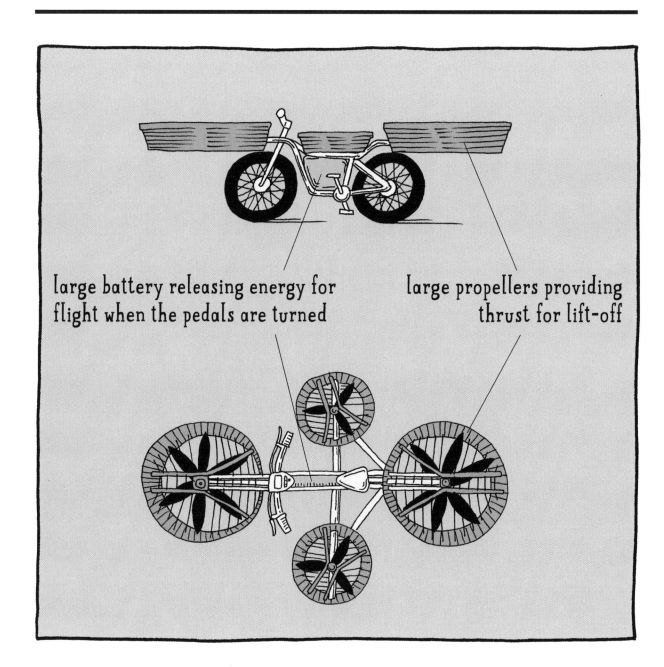

large battery releasing energy for flight when the pedals are turned

large propellers providing thrust for lift-off

This design looks as if it could be anything from a mobile air conditioner to an eco-friendly cultivator, but it's actually a two-wheeled multicopter—in other words, a flying bicycle! The "FBike" was designed recently by seven Czech engineers. The first test flight, held in Prague, was successful, with a dummy

The smaller propellers help keep balance. Tilted to horizontal, they propel the vehicle forwards.

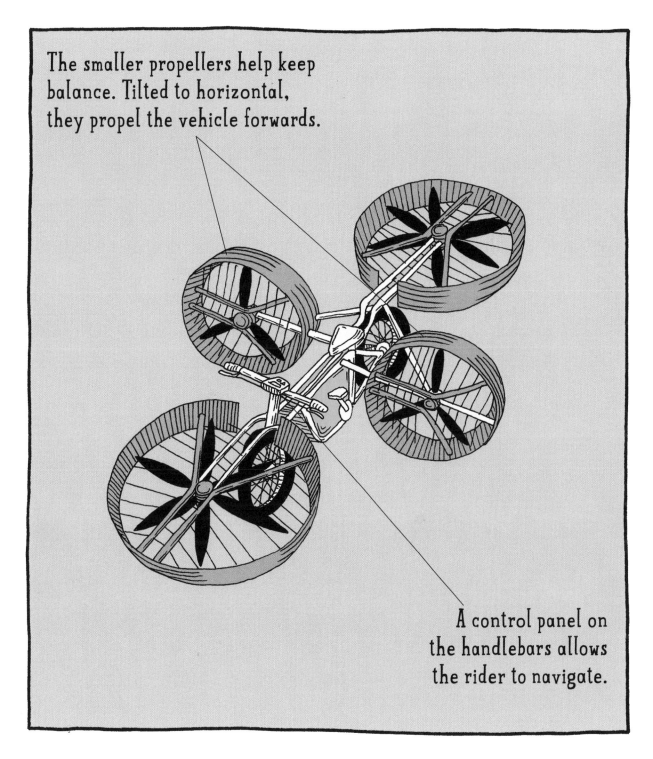

A control panel on the handlebars allows the rider to navigate.

at the handlebars landing safely after a few minutes of flight.
The bike is not yet capable of safely supporting a rider so it's controlled remotely.

And there's another problem: the battery lasts for only three to five minutes. That gives you time to fly over a traffic jam, but would it be it worth the trouble?

91

Leggy Locomotive

Why would a steam engine need a pair of legs? During the Napoleonic Wars, the price of horse feed rose as armies had tens of thousands of horses to feed.

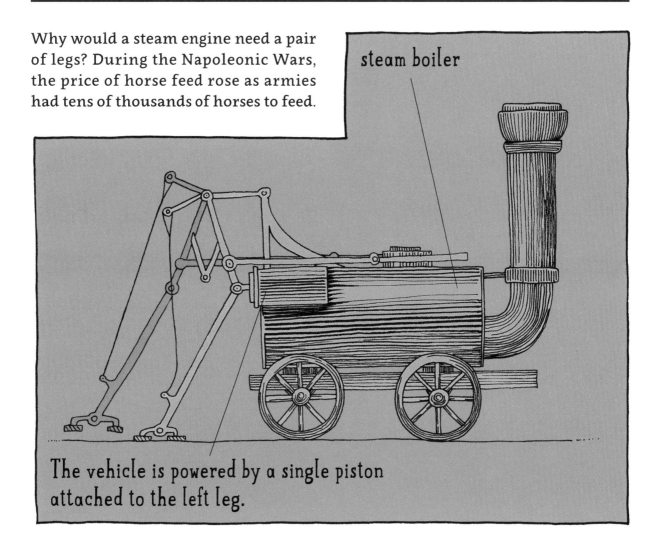

steam boiler

The vehicle is powered by a single piston attached to the left leg.

This hastened the transition from horse-drawn vehicles to steam-powered engines. William Brunton, a Scottish engineer and inventor, came up with one of the first, a locomotive with legs. He designed two models—both enormously heavy with the larger one weighing as much as three cars. It was thought that wheels alone would not grip the rails firmly enough on steep inclines, so the legs would help push the locomotive uphill. Brunton hoped his invention would replace the thousands of horses working in coal mines across the country. Everything was going well until a boiler full of hot steam exploded during a presentation of the vehicle, killing and injuring many spectators.

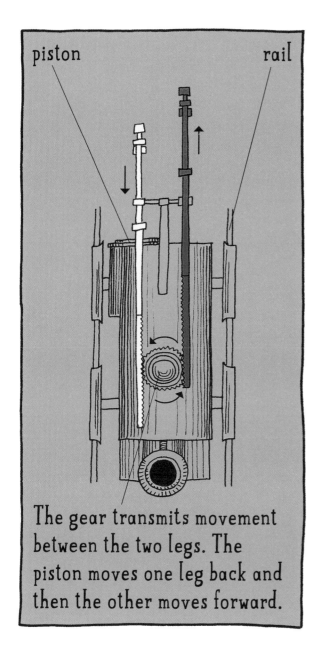

piston   rail

The gear transmits movement between the two legs. The piston moves one leg back and then the other moves forward.

This catastrophe, effectively the first railway disaster, also put an end to the locomotive with legs.

Today, similar constructions are found in robots and specialized walking machines used in industry. Sometimes even the zaniest idea comes back to life centuries later in a new guise.

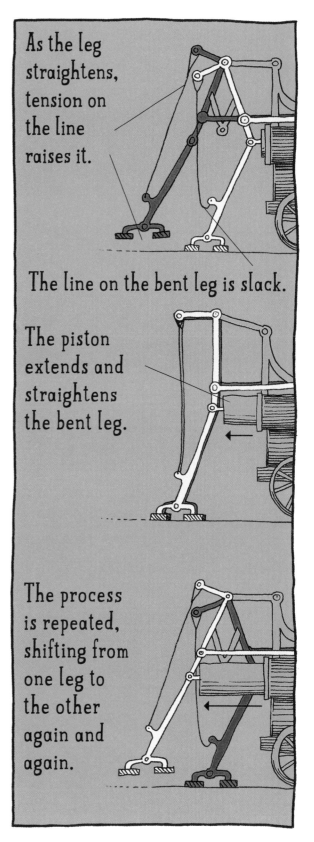

As the leg straightens, tension on the line raises it.

The line on the bent leg is slack.

The piston extends and straightens the bent leg.

The process is repeated, shifting from one leg to the other again and again.

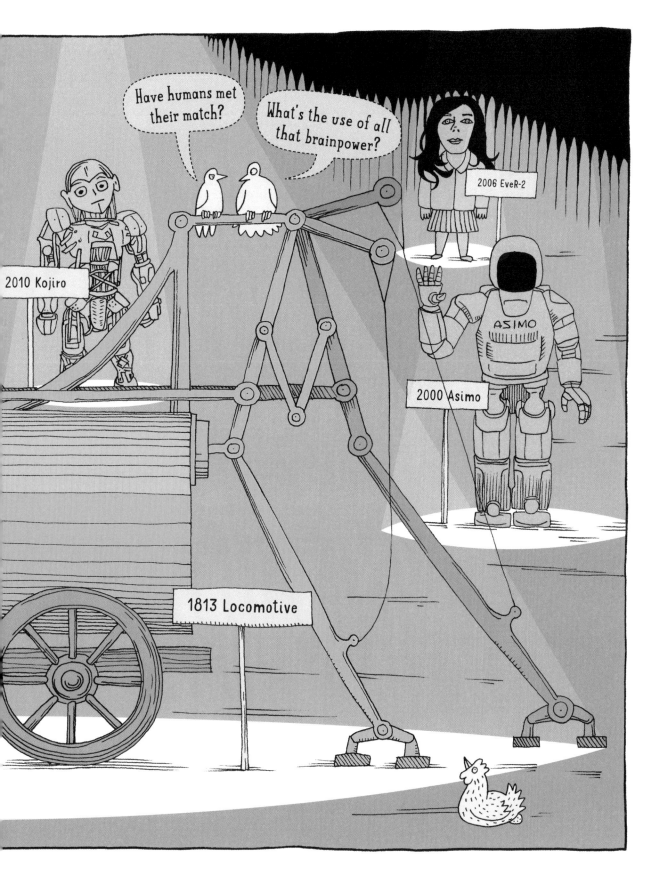

Magnetic Balloon

A sheep, a duck and a rooster: these were the passengers in the first hot air balloon flight in France in 1783. The menagerie landed safely and Europe went wild over the invention. Balloons were successfully flown in France, Italy and England over the following months, with people taking the place of the first animal passengers.

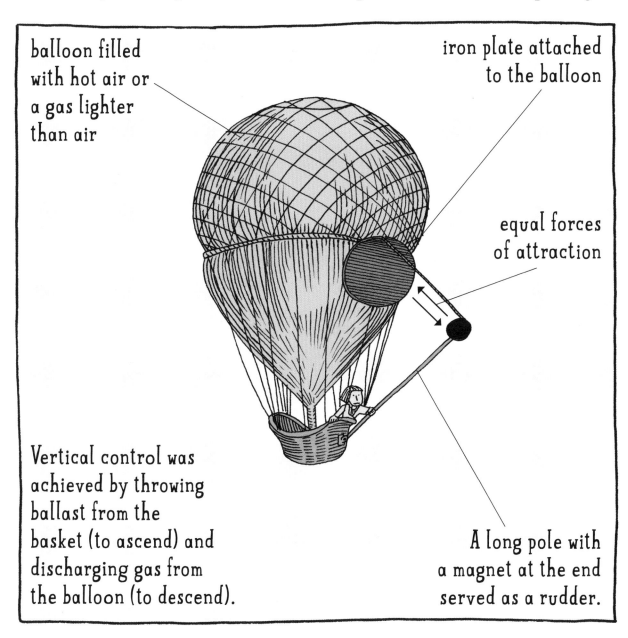

balloon filled with hot air or a gas lighter than air

iron plate attached to the balloon

equal forces of attraction

Vertical control was achieved by throwing ballast from the basket (to ascend) and discharging gas from the balloon (to descend).

A long pole with a magnet at the end served as a rudder.

But a balloon was hard to control and could land anywhere. Driven by the wind, it simply drifted across the sky until it caught on a treetop or church spire, or sank when the balloon ran out of fuel and cooled. Ballooning came to be considered pricey and dangerous fun. So inventors racked their brains over how to make ballooning cheaper and safer.

He showed his proposal to the king, who was delighted with it and sent it to scholars in Berlin and St Petersburg. They shook their heads in dismay. How could you drive a vehicle and be a passenger at the same time? They argued that since the magnet would attract the iron plate, and the iron plate would attract the magnet, the forces would

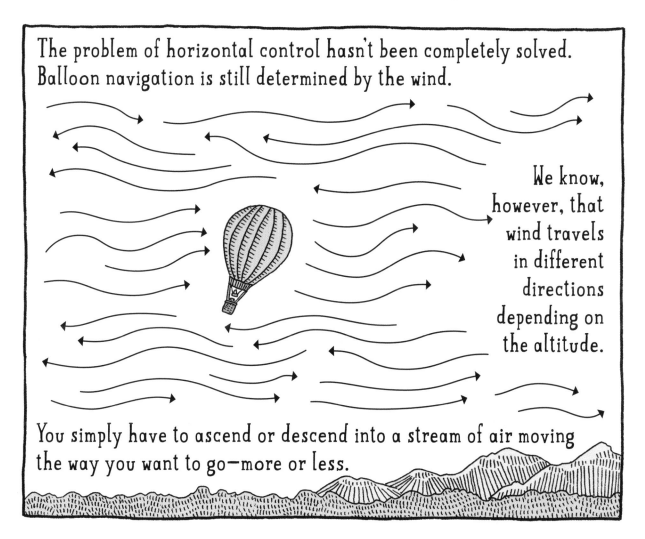

The problem of horizontal control hasn't been completely solved. Balloon navigation is still determined by the wind.

We know, however, that wind travels in different directions depending on the altitude.

You simply have to ascend or descend into a stream of air moving the way you want to go—more or less.

One of the most promising ideas came from Stanisław Trembecki—a Polish poet—which used the laws of magnetism to steer the balloon.

cancel each other out. The balloon would go nowhere. The scholars advised that Trembecki leave inventing to others and stick to poetry.

98

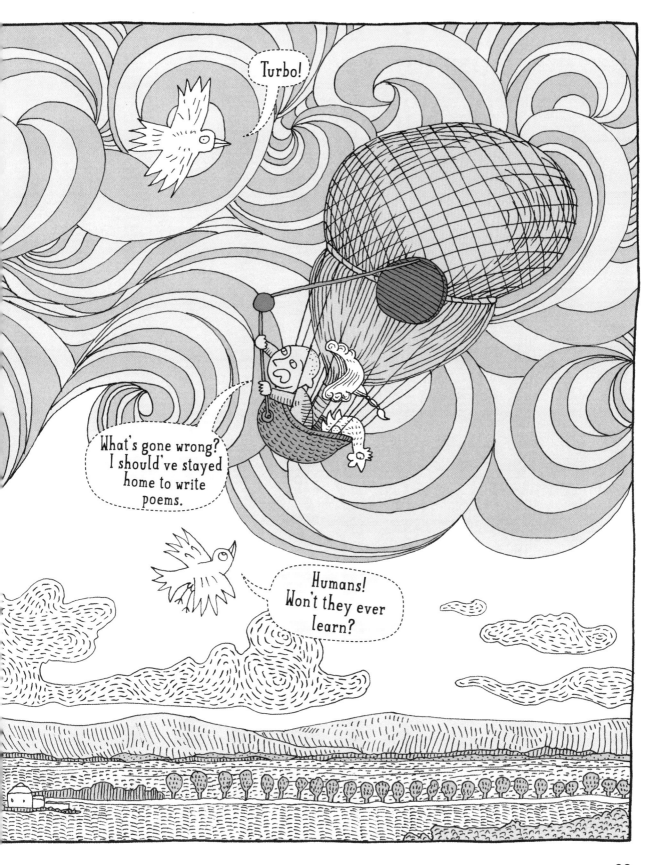

Sweet Sorter

An old telescope, a bird feeder, ceramic bowls and a sensor that measures the amount of red, green and blue. Throw in some epoxy resin and what do you get?

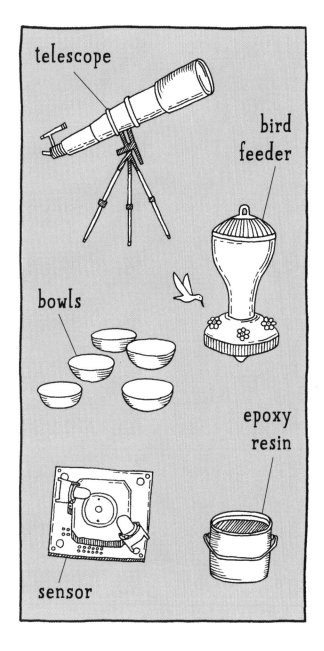

telescope

bird feeder

bowls

epoxy resin

sensor

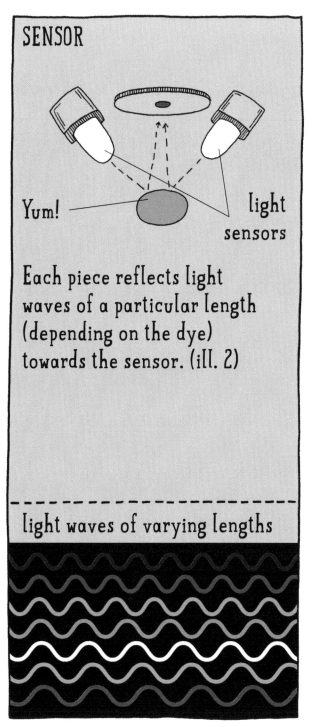

SENSOR

Yum!

light sensors

Each piece reflects light waves of a particular length (depending on the dye) towards the sensor. (ill. 2)

light waves of varying lengths

Well, probably any number of things, but this sorter invented in 2010 by the American artist and engineer Brian Egenriether is a concept especially for picky eaters.

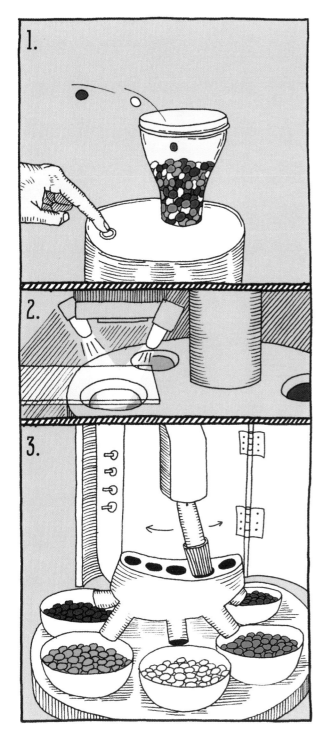

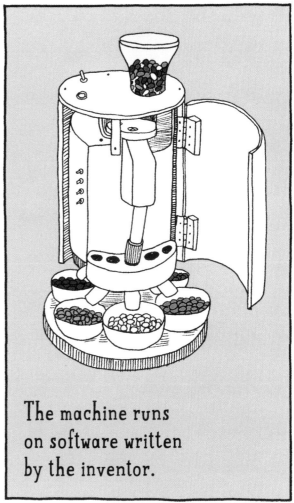

The machine runs on software written by the inventor.

The sorter can identify and separate sweet treats by their artificial dyes. The sensor measures the difference between red, green, orange and so on. It then sends an appropriate signal to the motor-controlled spout, which moves to drop each one into the right bowl.
The machine is made mostly of epoxy resin, a substance that's both flexible and durable when it sets. All of the other parts—the bird feeder, bowls, screws, wooden base, and hinges—were found lying around the inventor's shed.

Hotpot Automobile

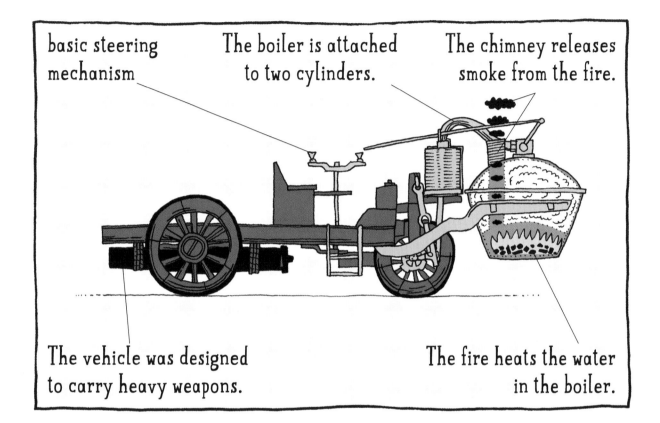

basic steering mechanism

The boiler is attached to two cylinders.

The chimney releases smoke from the fire.

The vehicle was designed to carry heavy weapons.

The fire heats the water in the boiler.

No, this isn't a diagram of the world's first food-delivery system. The pot was a boiler at the front of the vehicle producing steam to propel it. The *fardier à vapeur* ("steam dray") was the great-great-grandfather of today's car, invented by the French engineer Nicolas-Joseph Cugnot.

Alas, the vehicle wasn't very practical. The driver had to stop every fifteen or twenty minutes to relight the fire to keep it going. Also, it moved only at walking pace, tipped over easily and lacked a proper steering system. Nonetheless,

the inventor presented his machine to King Louis XV in 1771. He ended up losing control and crashing into a building. The incident went down in history as the first automobile accident. Government officials panicked and withdrew their funding for the project. Still, the king admired Cugnot for his efforts and offered him a lifetime income.

The machine is still around today, on display at the National Conservatory of Arts and Crafts in Paris. In 2010, French students made a working copy of Cugnot's invention, to prove it could be done.

Steam from the boiler expands, filling the left and right cylinders alternately, which powers the piston within.

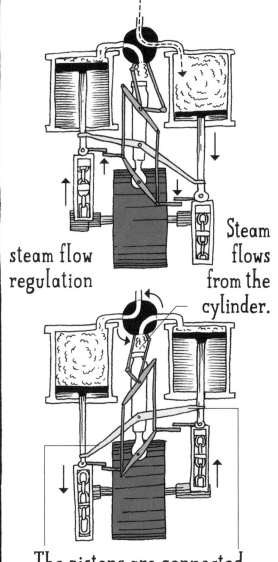

steam flow regulation

Steam flows from the cylinder.

The pistons are connected. As one is pushed out by the steam, the other is pushed in.

cogwheel

The opposite piston pulls the mechanism up.

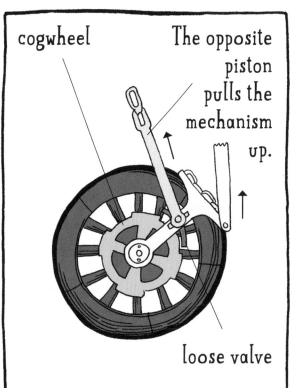

loose valve

The piston pushes the mechanism down and drives the front wheel.

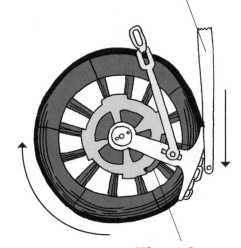

The valve grips onto the cog.

Championship Wings

It took people a few centuries to grasp that attaching wings to a person's arms won't allow them to fly. Human bodies are simply too heavy and weak. Luckily, modern technology helps us realize our high-flying dreams. Computers save time and money in aircraft development by helping to calculate, for example, the

Another ornithopter is shown on page 72.

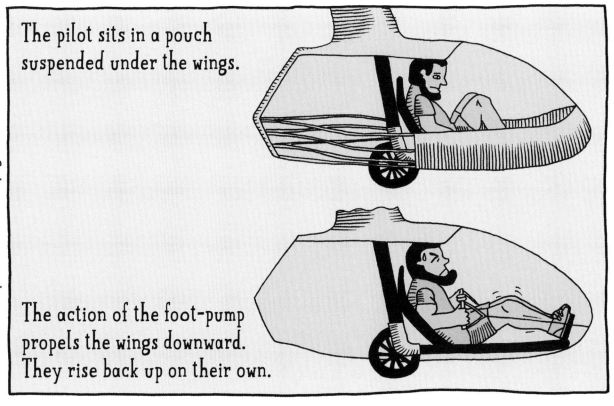

The pilot sits in a pouch suspended under the wings.

The action of the foot-pump propels the wings downward. They rise back up on their own.

The wings rotate during flight. The precisely calculated angle of the wings allows the Snowbird to move upward as well as forward.

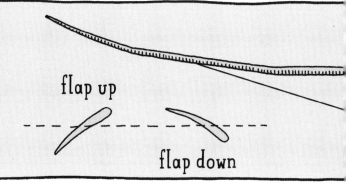

flap up

flap down

force needed for lift-off, and the best size and shape for wings.

A team of young inventors at the University of Toronto carried out a series of complex computer calculations to build their version of a modern-day ornithopter. Their invention, which they called the "Snowbird," is a fresh take on da Vinci's 15th-century idea. Best of all, it actually works. Made from lightweight materials, it weighs as little as two mountain bikes.

When tested, the Snowbird didn't fly very far or fast, or for very long, but it broke the world record for sustained flight of a human-powered aircraft. Today, the Snowbird is on display at the Museum of Aviation in Ottawa, Canada.

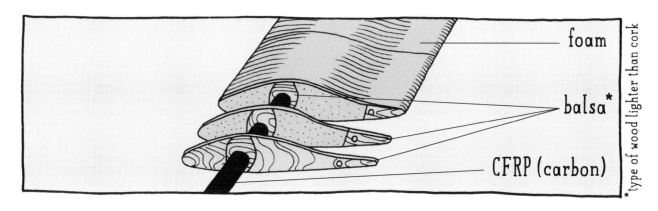

foam

balsa*

CFRP (carbon)

*type of wood lighter than cork

For the ornithopter to take flight, it has to be towed along like a huge kite.

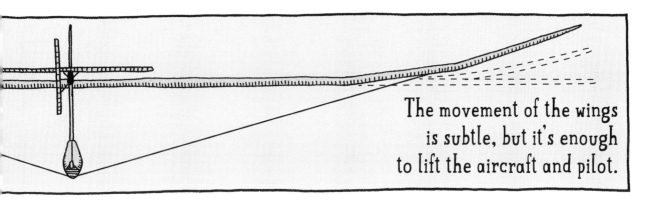

The movement of the wings is subtle, but it's enough to lift the aircraft and pilot.

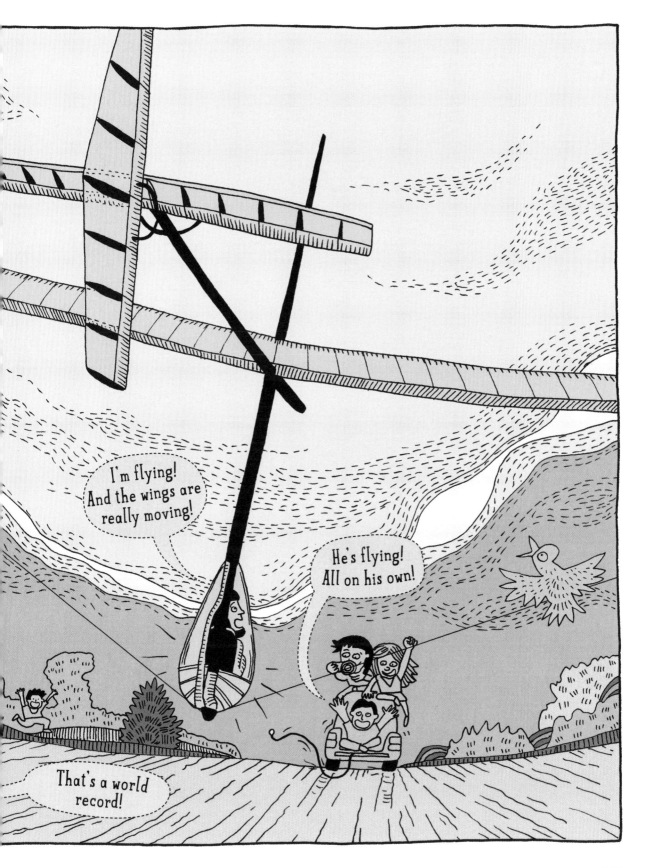

Ice Tunes

Today, many of us download our music online, but there are people who still love the scratchy, vintage sound of a phonograph record.

Ten of the ice-record-making sets were created to promote the single "Blue Ice" by the Shout Out Louds, an indie band from Stockholm.

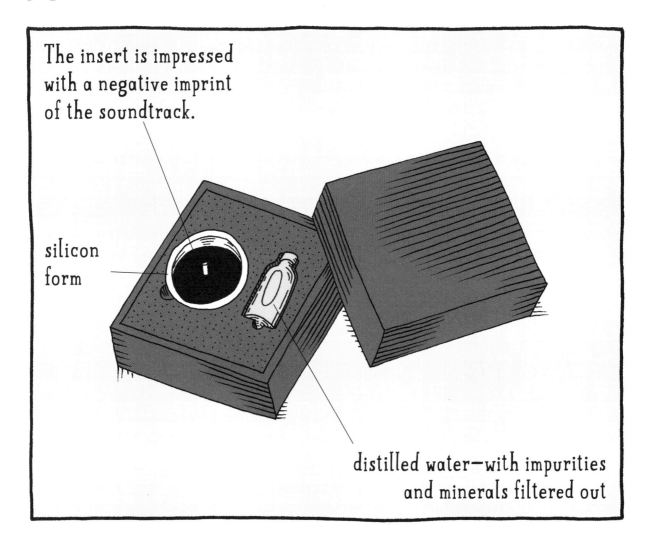

The insert is impressed with a negative imprint of the soundtrack.

silicon form

distilled water—with impurities and minerals filtered out

Swedish ad agency TBWA put a futuristic spin on old-fashioned turntable technology. They came up with a a way to cast an ice record that actually plays music.

The only trouble is it has to be played before the disc starts to melt. The upside? There's no risk of it getting scratched because you have a brand-new record

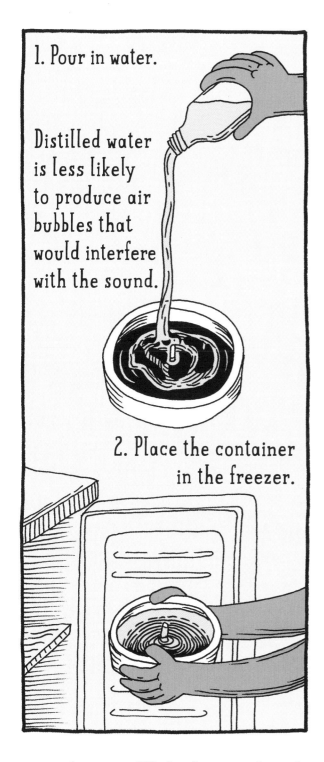

1. Pour in water.

Distilled water is less likely to produce air bubbles that would interfere with the sound.

2. Place the container in the freezer.

3. Take out after 4 hours.

4. Carefully remove the ice from the form.

5. Peel off the insert.

6. Get your record spinning and chill out.

every time you fill the form and put it back in the freezer. Four hours later, your disc is ready for another round. Now that is a cool invention!

3D Space Base

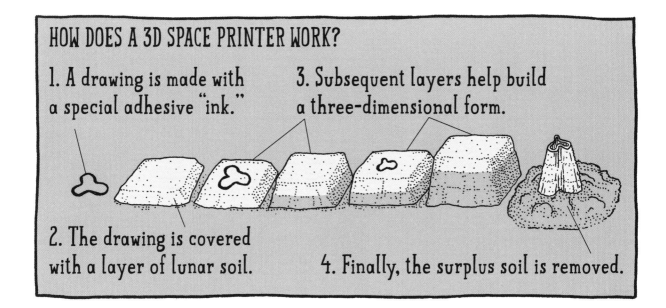

HOW DOES A 3D SPACE PRINTER WORK?

1. A drawing is made with a special adhesive "ink."

2. The drawing is covered with a layer of lunar soil.

3. Subsequent layers help build a three-dimensional form.

4. Finally, the surplus soil is removed.

Pretty soon, people are going to be able to build entire homes using 3D printing technology. On Earth, and even on the moon. Engineers at the London-based architecture firm Foster + Partners are working with the European Space Agency to create a small base on the sunlit side of the moon, using only a 3D printer.

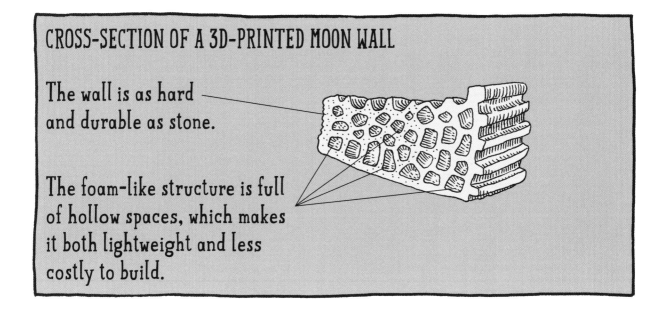

CROSS-SECTION OF A 3D-PRINTED MOON WALL

The wall is as hard and durable as stone.

The foam-like structure is full of hollow spaces, which makes it both lightweight and less costly to build.

BUILDING A MOON BASE

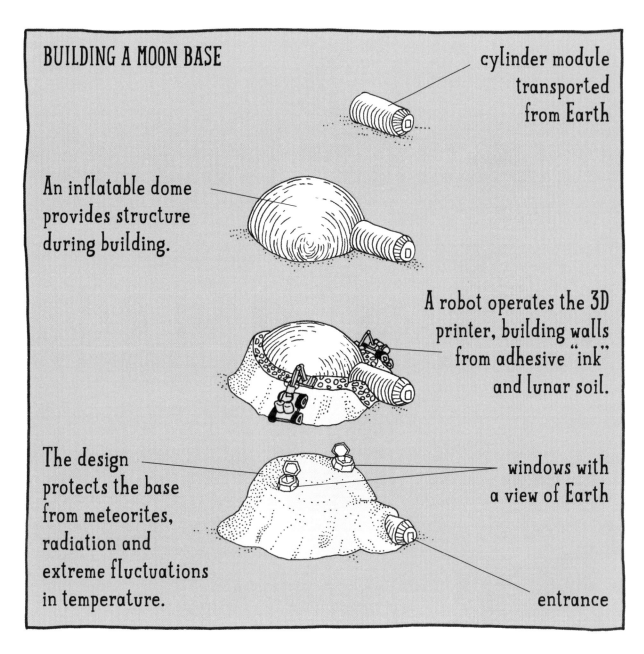

cylinder module transported from Earth

An inflatable dome provides structure during building.

A robot operates the 3D printer, building walls from adhesive "ink" and lunar soil.

The design protects the base from meteorites, radiation and extreme fluctuations in temperature.

windows with a view of Earth

entrance

Is this really possible? Yes! And it's cost-effective, too, because instead of transporting the building components through space, the printer can use local materials. In this case, the material is regolith—the dusy soil that coats the moon's surface. And with robots doing the hard work, humans won't have to exert themselves in the moon's harsh conditions of hot days, frozen nights and no oxygen. What's the point of building a moon base? Who'd want to live there? Surely lots of people dream of spending a night on the moon. Especially astronomers eager for unimpeded space exploration. Would you like to take part in a lunar sleepover?

Contents

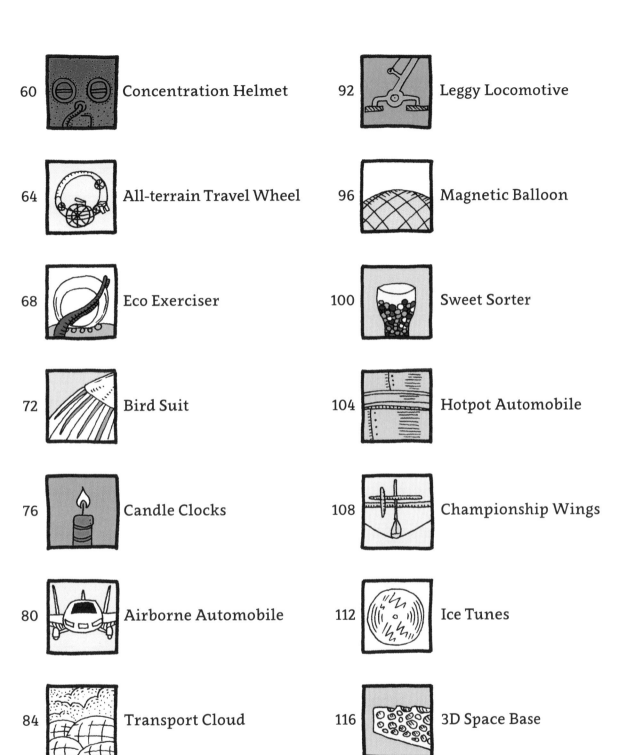

First American edition published 2018 by Gecko Press USA,
an imprint of Gecko Press Ltd.

This edition first published in 2017 by Gecko Press
PO Box 9335, Wellington 6141, New Zealand
info@geckopress.com

English-language edition © Gecko Press Ltd 2017
Translation © Agnes Monod-Gayraud 2017
Text © Wydawnictwo Dwie Siostry, Warsaw 2014
Illustrations © Aleksandra Mizielińska and Daniel Mizieliński 2014

Originally published in 2014 under the title *Ale patent!*
by Wydawnictwo Dwie Siostry, Warsaw.

Distributed in the United States and Canada by Lerner Publishing Group,
lernerbooks.com
Distributed in the United Kingdom by Bounce Sales and Marketing,
bouncemarketing.co.uk
Distributed in Australia by Scholastic Australia, scholastic.com.au
Distributed in New Zealand by Upstart Distribution, upstartpress.co.nz

This publication has been subsidized by the Polish Book Institute
© Poland Translation Programme

Edited by Penelope Todd
Design by Aleksandra Mizielińska and Daniel Mizieliński
Typesetting by Piotr Bałdyga
Printed in Poland

This publication has been supported by the ©POLAND Translation Program

For more curiously good books, visit geckopress.com

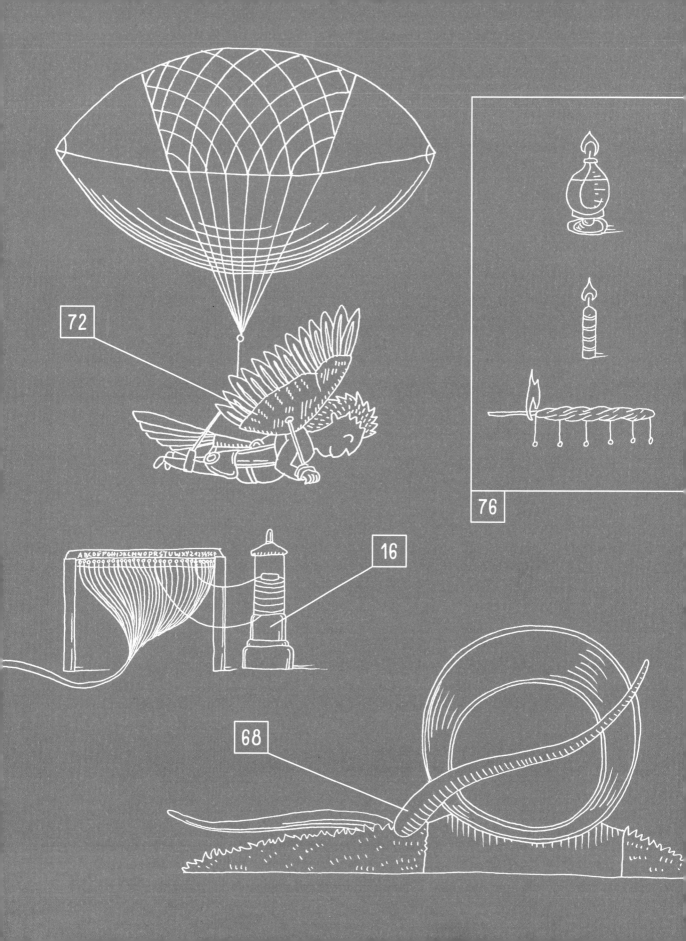